Killifish

First Steck-Vaughn Edition 1992

This book has been reviewed
for accuracy by
David Skryja
Associate Professor of Biology
University of Wisconsin Center—Waukesha.

Library of Congress Cataloging in Publication Data

Pohl, Kathleen.
  Killifish.

  (Nature close-ups)
  Adaptation of: Medaka / Sakaizumi Mitsuru.
  Summary: A description of various kinds of
killifish, their life cycles, and their behavior
patterns.
  1. Killifishes—Juvenile literature. [1. Killifishes]
I. Sakaizumi, Mitsuru. Medaka. II. Title.
III. Series.
QL637.9.A8P64 1986   597'53   86-26270

ISBN 0-8172-2720-2 (lib. bdg.)
ISBN 0-8172-2738-5 (softcover)

This edition first published in 1987 by Raintree Publishers Inc.,
a Division of Steck-Vaughn Company.

Text copyright © 1987 by Raintree Publishers Inc., translated by
Jun Amano from *Killifishes* copyright © 1981 by Mitsuru Sakaizumi.

Photographs copyright © 1981 by Hidekazu Kubo.

World English translation rights for *Color Photo Books on Nature*
arranged with Kaisei-Sha through Japan Foreign-Rights Center.

2 3 4 5 6 7 8 9 0   95 94 93 92

Killifish

Adapted by
Kathleen Pohl

RAINTREE
STECK-VAUGHN
LIBRARY
A Division of Steck-Vaughn Company

▶ **Killifish in spring.**

Killifish don't swim around much in winter. They stay still at the bottom of ponds and streams. But in spring, as the water becomes warmer, they become active. They begin to search for food near the water's surface.

◀ **Killifish in a river.**

These small, silvery fish swim together in groups called schools. Killifish are often called minnows, even though they do not belong to the minnow family.

Almost everyone who has been to a pond or stream has seen groups of small, silvery fish flashing through the water. These are called minnows. They are commonly used as bait by many fishermen. There are more than 200 kinds, or species, of true minnows in the United States. They belong to the Cyprinidae family.

But not all of these small, silvery fish are true minnows. Some of them are killifish. They are similar to minnows in many ways, and are commonly called minnows by many people. But they are different enough to be placed by scientists in a different family, the Cyprinodontidae family. There are almost fifty species of killifish in freshwater ponds, lakes, and streams in the United States.

◄ A group of killifish in shallow water.

These killifish swim in sunlit water where water plants grow. Killifish eat both plants and animals. Young killifish, especially, eat plankton, tiny bits of plant and animal matter that float in the water.

► Killifish swimming near a crayfish.

Killifish are an important link in the food chain in ponds and streams. They eat insects and insect larvae that float in the water. In turn, killifish are eaten by larger fish, turtles, and other water animals.

Like many small fish, killifish usually swim together in groups, called schools. If a small school of killifish sees other killifish swimming in a bigger school, it will join them, making the school even larger. Swimming in schools helps protect killifish from enemies, or predators.

If you see small fish swimming in a school, how can you tell whether they are minnows or killifish? Killifish have a square or rounded tail fin, while a minnow's tail is forked. The killifish's back, or dorsal fin, is set back closer to its tail than is the minnow's dorsal fin. And the killifish's mouth is closer to the top part of its head than the minnow's is. This is because the killifish is a surface feeder. Its mouth tilts upward so it can easily reach food at the surface of ponds and lakes.

The body structure of a killifish.

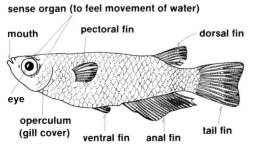

sense organ (to feel movement of water)

mouth   pectoral fin   dorsal fin

eye

operculum (gill cover)   ventral fin   anal fin   tail fin

► Small fish similar to killifish.

Killifish resemble true minnows in color and size. But they differ from minnows in the shapes of their tail fins and in the location of their dorsal fins and mouths.

Two species of minnows.

● **A killifish fighting over his territory (upper photos page 8 and page 9).**

Killifish in ponds and streams do not fight over territory. But if they are placed in a smaller space, in a tank or aquarium, some males will try to establish a territory by fighting off other males.

Because killifish are so small, only an inch or two long, many of them can live together in the same pond or stream. They don't need a lot of space, or great amounts of food to eat. So, generally, killifish don't fight over space, or territory, as many other fish do, especially during the mating season.

During the mating season, it is easy to tell male and female killifish apart. The female's body becomes fat and bulging with eggs during this time. And, if you look closely at a male and female, you will see other differences, too. The male's dorsal fin is larger; it is also notched. His anal fin is also larger than the female's, and it is covered with tiny spines. The male's anal fin is yellow year-round. But the female's turns white when she is ready to lay her eggs.

▲ A male (bottom) and female killifish.

● **How to tell a male killifish from a female.**

The black arrows in the photo at the left show the large dorsal and anal fins of the male killifish. The diagram at the right compares the male and female dorsal and anal fins.

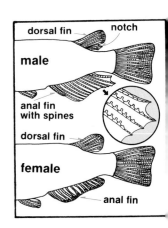

dorsal fin — notch

male

anal fin with spines

dorsal fin —

female

anal fin —

● **A pair of killifish mating (photos 1-5)**

When a female whose abdomen is bulging with eggs swims near a male, he follows her. He presses his body next to hers. The male discharges his sperm (see arrow, photo 4). Soon the female begins to release her eggs (photo 5).

Killifish do not go through elaborate mating rituals, like some kinds of fish do. When a female killifish with a bulging abdomen swims near a male, he follows her. He swims by her side and presses his body against her. The two fish head toward the bottom of the pond or stream. Soon the male releases sperm into the water through an opening in his body called a gonopore. Then the female discharges her eggs. When the sperm and eggs join together, the eggs become fertilized. Baby killifish soon begin to grow inside the eggs.

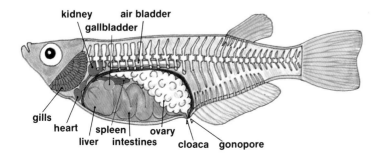

◀ The inside of a female's body.

The female's eggs develop in her ovary. The ovary becomes larger as the water temperature in the pond rises. By the time the female killifish is ready to lay her eggs, her ovary has enlarged so that it takes up more than half of her abdomen.

▲ **A killifish searching for a place to leave her eggs.**

The female swims with her fertilized eggs attached to her abdomen. She searches for a safe place to leave them.

▲ **A killifish depositing her eggs.**

The killifish leaves her eggs on several different leaves of this water plant.

▶ **A female killifish with her eggs.**

The fertilized eggs remain attached to the female killifish's abdomen as she swims through the water. She searches for a safe place to leave the eggs. If she finds a water plant, she will gently rub her abdomen against it, leaving some of the eggs. She may place the eggs on several leaves on the plant. If the female killifish can't find a water plant, she will shake her body in the water to release the eggs. Then she swims away and leaves the eggs to hatch on their own.

Many female killifish continue to mate and lay eggs throughout the summer. Some do so almost every day, laying ten to forty eggs at a time.

◀ **A female killifish discharging her eggs.**

First, the female bends her body (left), then she stretches it. This squeezes the eggs from her body (right).

The eggs are tiny at first, less than four-hundredths of an inch across. They are surrounded by a thin covering, a membrane. Tiny hairs on the membrane help the eggs stick to each other and to plant leaves.

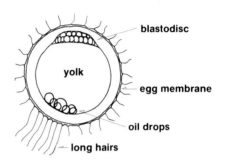

blastodisc

yolk

egg membrane

oil drops

long hairs

The egg is the life support system for the developing killifish, called the embryo. The egg case protects the embryo from water currents. And the egg yolk supplies nutrition for the developing killifish.

At first, the egg consists of a tiny single unit, called a cell. But soon, the cell divides in two, and then those cells divide, as well. This growth by cell division is essential because the killifish's body consists of billions of such cells. A tiny swelling, called the blastodisc, develops on the surface of the egg where the cells are dividing. Eventually, almost the entire surface of the egg yolk will be covered by the blastodisc.

▶ **The development of an embryo (photos 1-3).**

(1) Just a half a day after this egg was fertilized, many cells have already divided at the blastodisc (arrow). (2) Three days later, the embryo's head and long body can be seen through the egg case. (3) Four days later, the large black eyes and tiny blood vessels have formed.

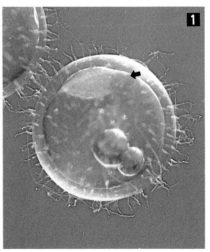

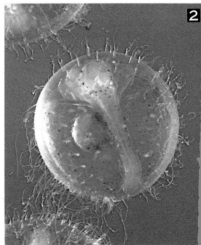

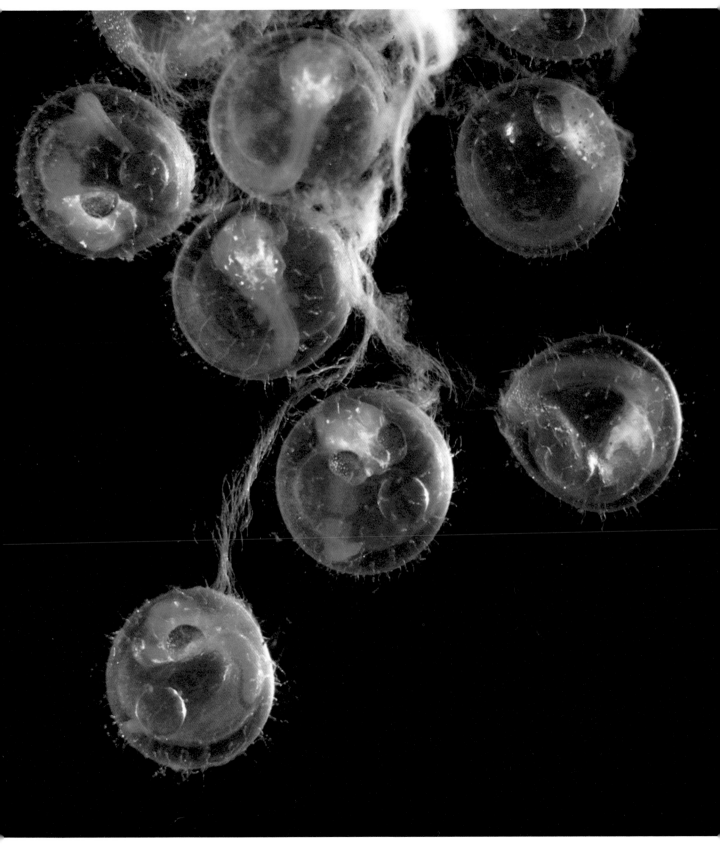

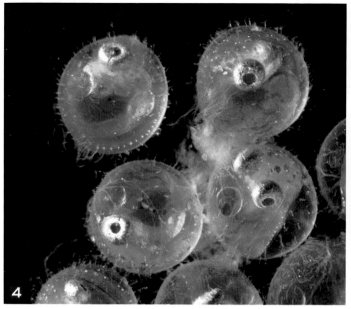

▲ Development of the embryo (photos 4-5).

By the time the embryo is a week old, the eyes are encircled by a silvery, glittering color. The tail continues to grow longer.

As the new cells continue to divide, the embryo grows rapidly. By the third day, its head and long tail have formed. Soon, its large black eyes become visible, and its heart begins to beat. Seven days after the egg was fertilized, the body of the embryo has almost completely formed. The black eyes are surrounded by a glittering silvery circle. Red blood cells can be seen through the transparent egg case.

The embryo continues to grow, but its shape does not change as much now as it did in the first few days. The tail grows longer, curving around in the egg case until it almost reaches the embryo's eyes. When the killifish embryo begins to move around inside the egg case, it is almost ready to hatch.

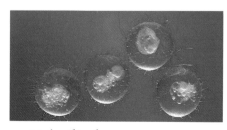

Unfertilized eggs.

Moldy eggs.

◄ Unfertilized eggs.
Eggs which are not fertilized eventually die and become moldy. Even fertilized eggs sometimes grow moldy in the water.

► Embryos inside the egg cases.

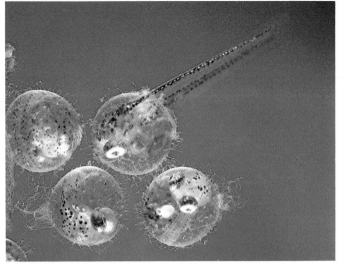

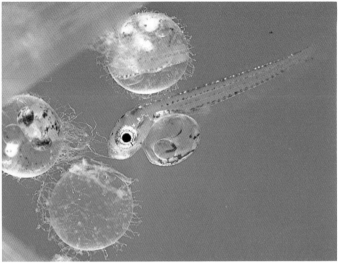

● **A baby killifish hatching (upper photos).**

The killifish produces a substance with its mouth that helps to dissolve the egg case. Most killifish break out of the egg case tail-first. Those that come out head-first usually die in the process.

▶ **A baby killifish swimming.**

The baby killifish is able to swim as soon as it has hatched. Some other kinds of fish fry are more helpless at first and must be cared for by one of the parent fish.

In about ten days, the killifish is ready to hatch. It secretes a special substance that helps to dissolve the egg case. Most killifish break out of the egg case tail-first.

The newly hatched killifish are called fry. The fry do not look at all like their parents at first. They have long tails, big heads, and the yolk sac remains attached to their bodies. The yolk provides the fry with nutrition so they don't have to look for food right away.

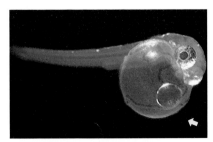 

A baby killifish taken out of an egg case (left) and one that hatched on its own (right).

◀ The baby killifish that hatched on its own has a longer tail. Its yolk sac is smaller because it has used up more nutrients. The one taken out of the egg case was not quite ready to hatch yet.

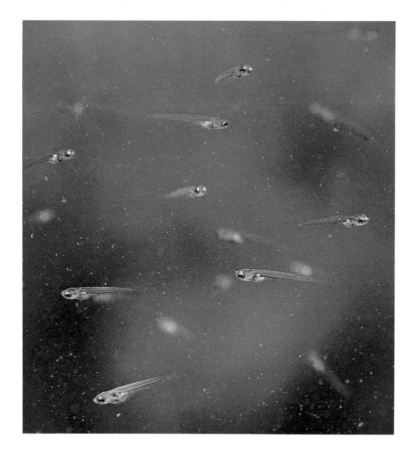

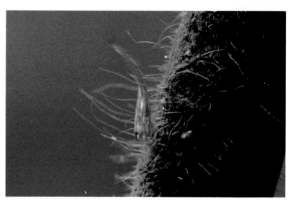

▲ **A young killifish eating pond scum.**

Some killifish fry eat pond scum. They also eat plankton and tiny insect larvae that live in the pond scum.

◄ **A group of killifish fry.**

► **A close-up view of plant and animal life in a pond.**

When the yolk sac is used up, the baby killifish begins to search for food on its own. At first, it eats mostly plankton, tiny bits of plant and animal matter that float in the water. Later on, it will eat various kinds of immature insects, called larvae, and adult insects.

But killifish fry are also in great danger of being eaten by fish and other underwater predators. Many fry do not survive this dangerous time in their lives. That is why so many killifish eggs are laid—it is nature's way of making sure that some killifish survive to become adults.

◄ **A river where killifish live.**

Throughout the summer, baby killifish are hatched from new batches of eggs that are laid by the adult killifish.

▶ **Other animals that are born in the water (photos 1-3).**

(1) A male giant water bug carrying eggs on his back (left) and a water bug nymph (right). (2) An adult shrimp scattering young shrimp into the water. (3) A pond snail giving birth (left) and a snail and its young (right).

At first, the baby killifish is tiny—only about one-quarter of an inch long. But as it eats, it grows rapidly. Within a month's time, it has grown to a half-inch. Its dorsal, caudal, and anal fins can be clearly seen. In three months, the young killifish of this species measures almost an inch long. It looks like an adult and will soon be mature enough to mate.

Meanwhile, the adult killifish in the pond will continue to mate throughout the summer, and many more baby killifish will be born. Many other animals in the pond, including giant water bugs, shrimp, and snails, also mate and reproduce during the summer months.

The growth of a killifish (photos 1-3).

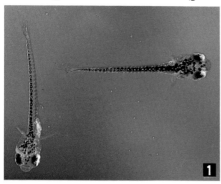

A newly hatched killifish.

A month-old killifish.

A three-month-old killifish.

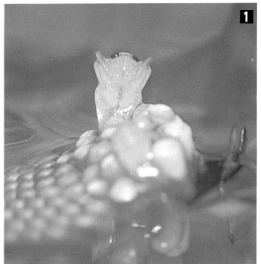

◄ **A school of killifish.**

Scientists have discovered that killifish eat more and grow faster when they stay together in schools. They also use less oxygen when they are together, than when they are by themselves.

► **Killifish nibbling at a piece of bread near the pond's surface.**

Killifish are omnivorous, which means they eat both plants and animals. They use their upturned mouths to catch insect larvae on the surface of the water. They also prey upon adult water insects and small crustaceans. Sometimes large killifish prey upon small killifish. Water plants, pond scum, and tiny green algae are all food sources for killifish.

Most fish have a good sense of smell, which helps them find food in the water. Killifish also have sense organs around their eyes. These detect movement in the water, alerting the killifish to insects and small animals swimming nearby.

► **A killifish's mouth.**

A killifish's mouth curves upward at the top of its head (left photo), making it easy for it to feed at the surface of lakes and ponds (right photo).

◄ A water scorpion watching killifish.

This water scorpion lies in wait for a killifish to swim nearby. When one does, the insect will reach out with its long, hooked front legs to catch its prey. Then it will use its needle-like mouth to pierce its victim and drink its body fluids.

► A Japanese wagtail searching for prey.

This Japanese wagtail keeps watch for small fish to swim near the water's surface.

Killifish play an important part in the food cycle of ponds, lakes, and streams. They help to reduce the insect population by eating many kinds of insects. In turn, the killifish population is controlled by other animals that live in the water. Large insects like water scorpions and giant water bugs prey upon killifish. Fish, turtles, and birds are also predators of the small, silvery fish.

The very young fry and the oldest killifish are the most likely to be eaten by predators. As they grow older, killifish cannot swim as fast as they once could, and so are more likely to be caught by enemies. Male killifish generally live longer than females. Some live five years or longer.

▲ A water scorpion that has seized a killifish.

▲ A giant water bug that has caught a killifish.

◄ **A river in winter.**

When winter comes, killifish cannot be found near the surface of lakes or ponds. The small fish hibernate beneath dead leaves or water plants until spring.

► **Killifish beneath dead leaves in a pond.**

Young killifish eat a lot during summer and fall. They do this instinctively to prepare for the coming winter. During winter they will not eat, but will live on energy stored in their bodies.

When the water begins to turn cold in the fall of the year, the female killifish stops laying her eggs. Like many pond animals, killifish go to the bottom of the pond or stream to spend the winter. They burrow beneath dead leaves or water plants and hibernate until spring. Their body functions slow down, and they live on energy stored in their bodies.

When the water begins to warm up in the spring, the killifish become active once again. They swim to the surface of the water and begin searching for food. Soon the mating season will begin again, and so the life cycle of the killifish continues.

A year in the life of a killifish.

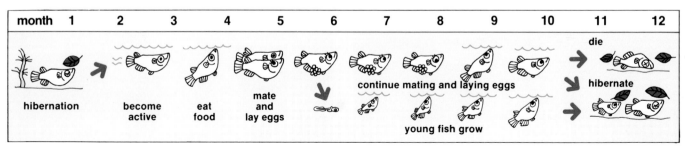

Let's Find Out How to Keep Killifish.

Place an aquarium in a sunny place. Fill it almost full with water. Put in both male and female killifish.

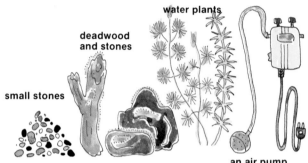

water plants

deadwood and stones

small stones

an air pump

How to Catch Killifish

Killifish move very quickly through the water, so be very quiet when you go near the pond. Scoop the fish up with a net. Be sure not to scoop up mud with the killifish.

nets

Food for the Killifish

Feed the killifish tropical fish food every day. Be sure not to overfeed them. Feed them live worms from time to time.

tropical fish food

water worms

midge larvae

A killifish eating water worms.

The Water for Your Aquarium

Warm the water in a sunny place for a day before putting it in your aquarium. Change half of the water every other week.

Warm the water with sunshine.

Change half the water twice a month.

▲ Killifish eating pond scum.

Let's Keep Killifish Eggs.

Killifish lay their eggs from May through August. Scoop up females that are carrying eggs on their abdomens. Gently place the eggs on a piece of paper and separate them. Place the eggs in a half-inch of water in a shallow dish. Change the water every day. Use a magnifying glass to watch the eggs develop. When the eggs hatch, place the young fry in a small water tank. Add some pond scum. Feed the fry small amounts of tropical fish food.

Place the eggs on a piece of paper and separate them.

Place the eggs in a dish with water.

Watch the eggs through a magnifying glass.

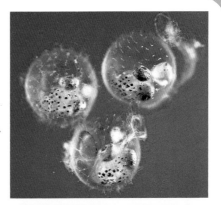

Eggs through which killifish embryos can be seen (upper) and a newly hatched killifish (lower).

A male killifish (below) and female (above).

The Killifish Family

The killifish that are sold at pet shops are closely related to killifish that are found in ponds and rivers. Guppies, swordtails, and gambusias are also closely related to killifish. They live in the warmer parts of the United States. But they don't lay eggs, as killifish do. They bear their young live.

A female guppy (below) and a male (above).

A male swordtail.

A male gambusia (middle) and two females.

GLOSSARY

cell—the basic unit of all plant and animal life. (pp. 14, 16)

egg—a mature female germ cell. (pp. 10, 12)

embryo—the early stages of development of a killifish or other organism. (pp. 14, 16)

fertilized—when a sperm and an egg unite, making it possible for a new organism to form. (pp. 10, 12)

fry—newly hatched fish. (pp. 18, 20, 22)

gonopore—the opening in the male killifish's body through which he releases his sperm. (p. 10)

hibernation—a period of inactivity undergone by animals during cold weather when their body functions slow down. (p. 28)

instinct—behavior with which an animal is born, rather than behavior which is learned. (p. 28)

plankton—tiny particles of plant and animal life that float in the water. (pp. 7, 20)

predators—animals that hunt and kill other animals for food. (pp. 7, 27)

school—a large number of fish of one kind swimming together. (pp. 4, 7, 25)

sperm—a mature male germ cell. (p. 10)

DATE DUE

NOV 05			
MAY 0 4 2009			
JUN 2 7 2001			
AUG 1 2 2009			
JUN 2 3 2011			
JAN 2 9 2013			
FEB 1 1 2013			
FEB 2 6 2013			
MAR 1 2 2013			